# Yule Fuel

*Cool Drama Scripts for Christmas*

by Jeff Smith

*Mary's Moment* conceived by Ron Jenkins and Jeff Smith.
*The Shepherd* originally conceived by Mason Smith.

Copyright © 2008 by Jeff Smith.
All print rights administered by Lillenas Publishing Co. All rights reserved.
Printed in the United States.

All scripture quotations are taken from the *Holy Bible, New International Version®* (NIV®). Copyright © 1973, 1978, 1984 by International Bible Society. Used by permission of Zondervan Publishing House. All rights reserved.

The purchase of this book entitles the purchaser to make photocopies of this material for use in their church or nonprofit organization. Sharing of the material in this book with other churches or organizations not owned or controlled by the original purchaser is prohibited. These scripts are protected by copyright. The contents of this book may not be edited, or reproduced in any other form without written permission from the publisher. Please include the above copyright statement on each copy made. Questions? Please write or call:

> Lillenas Publishing Company
> Drama Resources
> P.O. Box 419527
> Kansas City, MO 64141
> Phone: 816-931-1900 • Fax: 816-412-8390
> E-mail: drama@lillenas.com
> Web site: www.lillenasdrama.com

Cover art by JR Caines
Interior design by Tom Shank
Executive Editor: Kim Messer
Copy Editor: Kimberly Meiste
Manuscript Formatting: Karen Phillips

# Dedication

My father's family taught me the value of hard work, an appreciation of nature, and a LOVE FOR CHRISTMAS. Living so far away from my family as an adult, my boys don't have the experiences I had at Christmastime; I don't know what their stories will be to pass on to their children, but I have tried to pass on the love of Christmas that my father's side of the family passed on to me. For that, I want to dedicate this collection of Christmas sketches to my father's family:

Elder Clair and Luella Smith

Don and Jean Rook

John and Ruth Smith

Don and Karen Smith

Dick and Pam Smith

I've always said that "the imagination in a child is the seed of faith in an adult."

*"I Believe"*

Jeff Smith

# Contents

Comfortable with Joy . . . . . . . . . . . . . . . . . . . . . . . . . . . . . . . . . 7

All Strung Up . . . . . . . . . . . . . . . . . . . . . . . . . . . . . . . . . . . . . . . 9

Walking in Darkness . . . . . . . . . . . . . . . . . . . . . . . . . . . . . . . . 11

The Two Minute Drill . . . . . . . . . . . . . . . . . . . . . . . . . . . . . . . . 15

The Red Zone . . . . . . . . . . . . . . . . . . . . . . . . . . . . . . . . . . . . . . 22

Second Chances . . . . . . . . . . . . . . . . . . . . . . . . . . . . . . . . . . . . 25

Black Friday . . . . . . . . . . . . . . . . . . . . . . . . . . . . . . . . . . . . . . . 28

Simeon . . . . . . . . . . . . . . . . . . . . . . . . . . . . . . . . . . . . . . . . . . . 31

A Carpenter's Rule . . . . . . . . . . . . . . . . . . . . . . . . . . . . . . . . . . 34

Mary's Moment . . . . . . . . . . . . . . . . . . . . . . . . . . . . . . . . . . . . 37

The Shepherd . . . . . . . . . . . . . . . . . . . . . . . . . . . . . . . . . . . . . . 39

The Innkeeper's Wife . . . . . . . . . . . . . . . . . . . . . . . . . . . . . . . 42

The Christmas Narrative . . . . . . . . . . . . . . . . . . . . . . . . . . . . . 44

# Comfortable with Joy

**Running Time:** 2 minutes

**Themes:** Stress, Worship, Peace

**Scripture Reference:** Colossians 3:15

**Synopsis:** A family of three joins in the congregational singing of the traditional hymn, *God Rest Ye Merry, Gentlemen*. But what we hear is what they are thinking and not the words of the hymn. So much drama in one short song! What are these people thinking anyway?

**Cast:**
  BRENDA—Soccer mom/wife, 30+, has a busy to-do list and is stressed over Christmas planning and preparations
  TED—Distracted father, 30+, trying to avoid a confrontation with his best friend after accidentally wrecking his car
  ANGIE—Socially conscious teenage (14) daughter who likes to text friends

**Props:**
  2 Hymnals
  Small notepad with pencil
  Purse
  Cell phone

**Setting:** A pew/chairs in a church during the worship service

(TED, BRENDA, and ANGIE *are a small family of three attending church during Advent. They are all distracted by issues outside the worship service, or in* ANGIE'S *case, inside the worship service, but not part of worship! As the scene begins, they stand and open their hymnals to sing the traditional Christmas song,* God Rest Ye Merry, Gentlemen. *What we hear them sing, however, is their thoughts as opposed to the words of this blessed faith carol. When they are singing the actual words to the carol or when they are not "thinking" out loud, they should be pretending to sing the words of the hymn.* ANGIE *never actually picks up a hymnal until the very end. She is texting her friend.*)

ALL: "God rest ye merry, gentlemen; Let nothing you dismay."

BRENDA: I wonder if that Smell-Be-Gone comes in a scrub or spray?

ANGIE: I think that's Joy Wainright who's sitting next to Tyler Ray!

TED: Oh, I wonder what Gregory will say?

ALL: Gregory say . . .

TED: When I tell him that I wrecked his Chevrolet.

ALL: "From God, our heav'nly Father, a blessed angel came."

BRENDA: That little pile the puppy left is going to leave a stain.

ANGIE: I've got to text Felicia, isn't Amber Tyler's flame?

TED: Oh, I wish there was someone else to blame.

ALL: Someone to blame . . .

BRENDA: And we just put down new carpet. What a shame.

ALL: "Fear not, then," said the angel; "Let nothing you affright."

BRENDA: Having a puppy in the house makes me a bit uptight.

ANGIE *(texting)*: G-F, O-M-G, You will never guess what's in my sight. T dot Ray n-x-t-2 J. Wainright.

ALL: They're looking tight . . .

TED: I'll return it in the middle of the night.

ALL: "The shepherds at those tidings rejoiced with much in mind,"

TED: I'll back it in so he can't see the damage from behind.

ANGIE: Here's my 0-2, B-F is through, his game is undermined.

BRENDA: You just never can tell what you will find . . .

ALL: What will you find . . .

BRENDA: When you go away and leave your dog behind.

*(As they get ready to sing this last verse, BRENDA reaches over and points to ANGIE'S phone as if to tell her to put it away.)*

ALL: "Now to the Lord sing praises; All you within this place,"

BRENDA: Oh Lord, I didn't put down any paper in his cage.

ANGIE: T-T-F-N, and G-2-G, a parent on my case. *(Huffs and puts the phone away)*

TED: Yes, he knows! I can see it in his face. I'm a disgrace!

*(TED moves out of the pew area hiding behind his hymnal so as not to be seen. BRENDA, who has obviously been distracted by thinking about the dog, puts down the hymnal and exits in the opposite direction in a panic. ANGIE watches both of her parents leave suddenly and then pulls out her cell phone and begins to text again.)*

ANGIE: Looks like, Tyler Ray is comfortable *(comf-ter-bull)* with Joy.

*Blackout*

# All Strung Up

**Running Time:** 3 minutes

**Themes:** Evangelism, Witnessing, Joy, Stress, Worship

**Scripture Reference:** Matthew 5:14-16

**Synopsis:** A woman working in retail can't get a string of Christmas lights to work, only to be gently reminded that her bad attitude is keeping her light from shining in the workplace; a sketch about finding joy in the season.

**Cast:**
>   DIANE—A 30+ seasonal hire at a Christmas store during Christmas, responsible for decorating the trees in the Christmas shop

**Props:**
>   A string of white Christmas lights
>   Table(s) and chair
>   Cell phone

**Setting:** A break room in the back of a Christmas store

**Production Notes:** Staging is very simple. The scene only requires a chair onstage, but you can add a table and other props or set pieces that would imply a break room. If there is no outlet onstage, I recommend that you connect the lights to an extension chord that will reach to the chair. The string of lights needs to be able to "come on" when the new bulb replaces the bad one. As an option, you may leave one socket empty or just pretend like you're changing out the bulbs and have someone offstage plug the lights in so that they turn on at the appropriate time in the script. The use of an ellipse in the script (. . .) signifies a pause in the monologue and indicates a response from Carol on the other end of the line.

(DIANE *enters the room draped in a string of Christmas lights hanging over her shoulder and nearly all the way to the floor on each end. One of the lights in the string is bad and she must try to replace it. She is obviously frustrated and a little disheveled from a difficult day at work. She plops herself down on the chair and sighs. As she begins to go through the string of lights, her cell phone rings.*)

DIANE: Hello . . . Hey, Carol . . . Oh, I'm just about at the end of my rope; literally . . . I mean, I'm at the end of a string of Christmas lights that aren't exactly working and I'm trying to figure out what the problem is. I think it's a bad bulb. I had the tree almost completely finished . . . oh, the Cherub Tree . . . Yeah, white and gold; strung with white pearls, with angel feathers, hand made crocheted angel doilies . . . yeah, beautiful until I had to rip it apart and start over again. God created the universe faster than it's taken me to decorate that tree. So what's up? . . . *(Exasperated)* Oh, no! I totally forgot . . . I know! I know it's not the first time. But, I can't be at worship practice tonight. I won't finish this until at least 9:00 . . .

9

Oh, it was so much easier when it wasn't my job, you know? I always loved decorating for Christmas. I'd start in October setting up trees in all the rooms of the house, decorating hallways, dressing windows. We had friends over . . . (*Laughs*) Yes, I had friends then, Miss Sarcastic. You came over and we'd have our baking day, remember? Horns, gingerbread cookies, nut rolls . . . uh-huh and cinnamon and clove simmering on the stove. We'd sing Christmas carols . . . *don't* sing *Oh Tannenbaum* to me right now! That's not funny . . .

We need the money at Christmas. I mean, Bob's salary doesn't give us enough to spend on the kids for the holidays. And I loved decorating. It seemed like a great fit. Where did the joy go? (*Pause*)

Part of it is the store owner. I call her Matilda the Hun. What an ogre . . . My witness? You have no idea! You remember that "Great Outdoors"-theme we decorated one tree last year? . . . Right; the fisherman, hunter, wild animals . . . that's the one. She made me take it apart because she said the lights weren't even. I almost told her to take a hike!

Then, she said Rudolf's nose was more coral red than scarlet red and so I had to change out all of the 'scarlet red' Christmas ornaments on the tree to match. Hello? That's one shade of red in the entire color spectrum. I mean, who cares? . . . What would Jesus do? Oh, I tell you what he'd do. He'd come in here and turn everything in this store upside down like he did with the money changers in the temple. He would say, the whole thing was way too commercial and we needed to get back to the real meaning of Christmas! . . . All right, I'm sorry. I'm just so stressed. Yeah, yeah, we're supposed to be salt and light; salt and . . .

(DIANE *replaces a bulb and the whole string of lights comes on.*)

*Light*! Got it . . . No, I mean, the string of lights is working. I found the bad bulb. It figures that it would be right at the end of the string. Hmmmph. I should have started at this end. I've got to run. Sorry about worship tonight . . . OK.

(DIANE *hangs up the phone and puts it back in her pocket. She looks at the string and the bulb she just replaced. She talks to it like a thief that stole her joy.*)

It's all your fault that the rest of these lights weren't working. Just because you were bad, the whole string doesn't work.

(DIANE *stops to consider something that she hadn't considered until now. Perhaps she replaces the good bulb with the bad bulb again and watches the string turn off and then back on.*)

"Let your light shine before men, that they may see your good deeds and praise your Father in heaven."

(DIANE *pulls out the cell phone and calls Carol.*)

Carol? . . . Hey, it's me again. Thanks for being such a good friend . . . Just not being afraid to say what I needed to hear. Listen, I'll be there tonight . . . It'll work out. And I think I'm going to invite Matilda, the . . . I mean, Mrs. Hoover, to the church Christmas play *after* I apologize for my bad attitude . . . What happened? (*Pause*) I saw the light!

# Walking in Darkness

**Running Time:** 5 minutes

**Themes:** Hard heartedness, Bitterness, Reconciliation

**Scripture References:** Luke 2:7; Hebrews 3:15; Revelations 3:20

**Synopsis:** "Peace on earth and goodwill towards men" is still a long way off, even 2,000 years after the birth of Christ. Matthew 10:34 says, "I did not come to bring peace, but a sword!" The power of these words is captured in this sketch about two brothers who get caught in the crosshairs of Christmas.

   The birth of the Messiah brings two brothers together after an awkward separation; one is a wayward shepherd that tends a small flock in the hills of Judea and the other a respected innkeeper from Bethlehem. Peace on earth and goodwill towards men is still a long way off; a sketch about hard-heartedness and pride.

**Cast:**

   DANIEL—Younger brother, 30+, the black sheep of the family; shepherd

   ELIAS—Older brother, 35+, responsible and deeply scarred; innkeeper at Bethlehem

**Props:**

   Linens
   Towels
   Rags
   Lanterns (a couple)
   Wooden bucket
   Broom
   Stool

**Setting:** A service room or area in the infamous Bethlehem Inn.

**Production Note:** The piece should be played in period. The language and specific setting doesn't work well in an anachronistic light. This infers biblical costumes and set pieces that are appropriate.

*(As they enter the room, DANIEL is sharing some exciting news with his older brother, ELIAS, about angels that appeared to him and the other shepherds in the night. ELIAS is only partially engaged as he is obviously very busy and preoccupied with sorting and folding linens and checking off [at least mentally] things he has to do. He is also checking oil in lamps and counting a small bag of coins. It is an unusually busy and very hectic night at the Bethlehem Inn. As ELIAS walks around the room gathering things and putting things in order, DANIEL is following him around the room like a puppy. At least once, they should bump into each other.)*

ELIAS: Uh, so you were saying something about an angel?

DANIEL: Actually, I saw a lot of angels. There was a big one and then there were a lot of little ones.

ELIAS: And what were these . . . angels . . . doing?

DANIEL: Well, they started off by saying, "Be not afraid."

ELIAS: You? Afraid? I can't imagine that.

DANIEL: Well, *yes*. I mean, I was on the hill watching the sheep in the middle of the night and all of a sudden it was as bright as day.

ELIAS *(counting linens):* Eight, nine . . . ten. What?

DANIEL: It was as bright as day.

ELIAS: Lamps. *(Walks over to check oil in a couple of lamps)*

DANIEL: Are you listening to me?

ELIAS: Yes, yes, brother; something about ghosts . . .

DANIEL: Angels.

ELIAS: Angels.

*(*DANIEL *takes a folded sheet, opens it, and puts it over his head like a long veil.)*

DANIEL: Angel. *(Speaks in broad and regal tones)* Do not be afraid!

*(He pulls sheet over his head.)*

DANIEL: Ghost. *(Bellows in a 'ghostly' sound)* Be afraid!

ELIAS: Get that off your head and refold it like you found it.

DANIEL: Sorry. I was just . . .

ELIAS: Don't start.

*(*DANIEL *takes off the sheet and refolds it.)*

ELIAS: Daniel, this isn't the first time you've seen things . . . on the hill . . . at night. When we were young shepherds you would see wolves that were just combinations of briar bushes and tree stumps. You saw thieves and it was nothing more than fence posts or shadows in a flickering fire. You see angels and my guess is that it's nothing more than overcooked porridge and lack of sleep or . . . strong drink!

DANIEL: But Elias, how could I mistake an angel . . . a heavenly host of angels, that filled the entire sky . . . with light . . . and music . . . at night?

ELIAS: Because you were afraid; you said so yourself. Fear can make people do crazy things.

DANIEL: Well, yeah . . . at first.

ELIAS: I remember when you would have dreams of the death angel that killed all the children at Passover. You'd wake up in a sweat in the middle of the night and you'd cry out for someone to save you. Our parents shouldn't have told us those stories.

DANIEL: Those stories are our heritage; Israel's hope.

ELIAS: Your hope is in stories about ghosts. My hope is my business. (ELIAS *shakes his head.*) Israel's deliverer!

DANIEL: But tonight, Israel is delivered from her nightmare. The Messiah has come.

(ELIAS *stops and looks at his younger brother. He walks over to him and sniffs his breath.*)

DANIEL: No, I haven't been drinking. I'm perfectly sane.

ELIAS: You've never been perfectly sane.

(ELIAS *starts to laugh.*)

DANIEL: What's the matter?

ELIAS: You. You're a shepherd. You drink. You live in the dark; in the desert. You're a ghost that flits in and out. (*Pokes his brother*) I don't even know if you're real. Then you come in here, after I haven't seen you in . . . how long . . . a year? And you tell me that you've seen angels and the Messiah has appeared . . . to you.

DANIEL: Why not? Haven't we waited long enough? Why not now?

ELIAS: Because I'm busy. Can't you see? I'm too busy for the Messiah tonight.

DANIEL: I guess so, because you put Him out in the back where you feed your animals.

(*Pause*)

DANIEL: Elias, the Savior of our people is asleep in your stable.

(ELIAS *stops with his activities. He sits on a stool. The following section should be delivered from opposite sides of the stage. Neither brother is really listening to the other. They are in their own separate worlds, talking to themselves. The lines can overlap or be spoken simultaneously.*)

DANIEL: The angel said, "I bring you good tidings of great joy. For unto you this day in the city of David, a Savior is born. He is Christ the Lord. And this shall be a sign unto you. You shall find a baby, wrapped in swaddling clothes, and lying in . . . a manger."

ELIAS: There was a couple . . . earlier tonight. The place was packed. Everybody needed something. It was impossible . . .

DANIEL: Old Jonas thought of it right away. The only manger he knew in all of Bethlehem that was under cover was right here.

ELIAS: She was pregnant, like she was going to deliver any moment. All I could think about was my Sarah . . .

DANIEL: So, we all got up and ran down here to see the thing the angel had spoken about.

ELIAS: We were so excited; our first. How we were looking forward to having a family. She was so good with children.

DANIEL: And when we got it here, it was just as the angel had said. There was a woman named Mary and her husband, Joseph. And there in the manger filled with straw was the most beautiful thing . . .

ELIAS: Screams in the night. I stood and paced. They wouldn't let me in. There was blood . . . they kept bringing out the rags covered with . . . the blood . . .

DANIEL: We bowed down and worshiped, this Holy One; the Christ; the Savior of God's people born here in Bethlehem, tonight, just as the prophets foretold.

ELIAS: And then . . . silence.

DANIEL *(turns to talk to* ELIAS*)*: Brother, you've got to come and see.

ELIAS: Dead silence.

DANIEL: What?

ELIAS *(picks up some linens and an oil lamp):* I've got paying customers that need my attention.

DANIEL *(incredulous):* You've got to do something. Can't you give them your room?

ELIAS *(sharply): My room*? I've already sold my room. *(Emphatically)* I have no more room. *(Pause)* I have paying customers that are walking around in the darkness. They need light and linens. Make yourself useful for once and take these to room 12.

*(*DANIEL *picks up a lantern and looks intently at it.)*

DANIEL: "Those walking in darkness have seen a great light. On those living in the land of the shadow of death, a light has come." Yahweh, help my brother and all here to see.

*(*DANIEL *exits.)*

# The Two Minute Drill

**Running Time:** 5 minutes

**Theme**: Unforgiveness

**Scripture Reference:** Colossians 3:13

**Synopsis:** A couple from Pittsburgh try working through their plans for Christmas day, but they seem to be going in different directions. Perhaps a little more teamwork is the goal. Add a referee, color commentators, and penalty flags and we have a real game going on! A tragedy-comedy about the added stress that Christmas can bring.

**Cast:**
> JEANNE HILTIBILTEY—Strong and independent, 30+ female. She's a paralegal assistant in a local law firm. Married to Ralph for 10 years, her marriage is superficial and troubled although she has been committed to working through it.
> RALPH HILTIBILTEY—Temperamental and sometimes distant, 30+ male. He's been slightly irresponsible in holding down a job. When he does achieve moderate success at work, he seems to self-destruct by drinking too much and getting himself in trouble.
> COMMENTATOR—Male/Female of 20+ years of age, non-descript; sports play-by-play analyst
> REFEREE—Male/Female of 20+ years of age, non-descript; very formal and official

**Props:**
> Referee flags or colored kerchiefs
> Bag of chips
> Bottle of beer or mug

**Setting**: Ralph and Jeanne's living room

**Production Notes**: Keep in mind that this piece requires specific focus:
- Ralph speaks to Jeanne and/or makes comments about the football game on the television as directed.
- The Commentator is providing analysis of the situation between Ralph and Jeanne using words and phrases that you would here on a television broadcast of a football game. Neither Jeanne nor Ralph can see or hear him/her. The Commentator does respond to calls made by the Referee onstage.
- The Referee is officiating the game being played between Ralph and Jeanne. But neither Jeanne nor Ralph can see or hear him/her.

Look for cues in the script as to where to direct focus and lines.

(RALPH *is sitting on a couch—facing the audience—watching a football game. He is drinking a beer and eating some chips from a bag. A man/woman dressed as* REFEREE *stands US of the scene. He is holding several red penalty flags. The* COMMENTATOR *is parked at a desk or podium SR of the scene. He/She can also be sitting on a stool.*)

COMMENTATOR: Welcome to the Home Improvement Network Television (HINT) and our continuing coverage of the National Marriage League. Today's match up promises to be a real doozy as Ralph and Jeanne Hiltibiltey of Pittsburgh, PA, try to overcome one of the strongest defenses in the game; a line up of over-sized prides. They're also fighting against offenses that have only gotten stronger and stronger with years of unforgiveness. Will they survive today's onslaught of the leagues toughest foes? We'll see if they're ready to fight back as we go down on the field for the opening kickoff.

(JEANNE *enters the room.*)

COMMENTATOR: Jeanne and Ralph line up for the opening kickoff.

JEANNE: We have to talk about Christmas this year.

COMMENTATOR: There's the kickoff and we're underway. Ralph takes the ball around his own twenty.

RALPH: Not now.

JEANNE: I have to make some plans.

RALPH *(emphatically):* Not now! The game just came on.

JEANNE: It will take two minutes.

RALPH: Jeanne, it's the Steelers versus the Browns. Wait 'til the break.

JEANNE: You give me a break. It's not like there's ever a good time to talk about this.

RALPH: OK. OK!

COMMENTATOR: He breaks a couple of tackles to the 30 and he's finally down at the 35. A modest gain. First down.

JEANNE: Martha wants us at your dad's for dinner at 12:00 *(motions the quotation marks with her fingers)* "sharp" this year and had the audacity to tell us not to be late again.

(REFEREE *blows a whistle and throws a flag.*)

REFEREE: False start on the offense. Five yard penalty. Second down.

COMMENTATOR: Ralph and Jeanne seem a little jittery here on the opening possession. Hopefully, they can get a rhythm going quickly. Second down and still a ways to go.

JEANNE: Ralph?

(JEANNE *clears her throat and looks away. She sighs like she is blowing off a little steam.*)

COMMENTATOR: Jeanne lines up over the ball again.

JEANNE: What do you want me to tell them?

RALPH: Tell them we'll do our best to get there at noon.

JEANNE: So we can what? *(Moves towards him)* Sit there and be miserable again while we wait for her to put dinner on the table at 2:30 P.M. and then be stuffed by the time we finally make it to my mother's . . . *late again* . . . because she didn't get up in time to start the turkey?

(REFEREE *blows a whistle and throws a flag.*)

REFEREE: There was forward motion before the snap. Five yard penalty. Third down.

COMMENTATOR: Third down and two penalties for ten yards. They're just getting started and already backed up deep in enemy territory. Jeanne and Ralph definitely need to connect here or they are three and out on their first possession of the game.

RALPH *(defiantly)*: What do you want *me* to do about it? *(Referencing the game and an apparent missed call by the* REFEREE*)* Oh, that was taunting on number 43, ref. I can't believe the ref missed that call!

[Note: If possible, RALPH *should be wearing a football shirt with a number that matches the number referenced above.*]

JEANNE: Ralph? We have to go to your mother's and then my family and then your father's all in the same day. We've been doing this for ten years. *(Softens)* You hate it as much as I do. *(Earnestly)* Honey please, can't we do something different this year?

COMMENTATOR: Nice hand-off. Ralph takes the ball and moves down the field.

RALPH *(turning to look at her)*: I do hate it and it is tough. What did you have in mind?

COMMENTATOR: Nice move. He dodges a defender and just barely gets the first down. That was a big gain. That gives them a chance to start again with a new set of downs. Let's see if they can start moving the ball.

(JEANNE *softens her stance or sits down.*)

COMMENTATOR: Jeanne takes the ball . . .

JEANNE: Why don't you call your dad and tell him we can't make it this year, and we'll see how it works out?

COMMENTATOR: She hands it off to Ralph . . .

RALPH: My dad? Why can't your mom back up dinner until 6:30 or 7:00?

COMMENTATOR: Sloppy. Ralph bobbled the ball there.

JEANNE: We already have to work around both sets of your parents. And, in case you've forgotten, we have a son who might like to get up and enjoy opening his gifts *at home* for a change.

COMMENTATOR: Blocked by the defense. Ralph is fighting to keep his feet underneath him.

RALPH: It's only one day out of the whole year, Jeanne.

COMMENTATOR: Was he out of bounds there?

JEANNE: It's Christmas.

RALPH: And what about the 364 other days I have to put up with your father living here?

(REFEREE *blows a whistle and throws a flag.*)

REFEREE: The runner clearly stepped out of bounds into unfair territory.

RALPH (*to the television set*): Out of bounds? You've got to be kidding me? He was ten feet inside the line. Throw the flag, coach.

COMMENTATOR: They are going to review the play to see if Ralph stepped out of bounds back at the line of scrimmage.

RALPH: Good call.

(RALPH *and* JEANNE *return to the exact spots they were in when they said, "We already have to work around both sets of your parents . . ." They recreate the scene word for word and motion for motion as if it is a "replay" of the scene through the supposed "infraction.")*

JEANNE: We already have to work around both sets of your parents. And, in case you've forgotten, we have a son who might like to get up and enjoy opening his gifts *at home* for once.

RALPH: It's only one day out of the whole year, Jeanne.

JEANNE: It's Christmas.

RALPH: And what about the 364 other days I have to put up with your father living here?

REFEREE: After reviewing the play, it appears that Ralph stepped on the line, but did not go over it. The ball will be marked at about mid-field. Second down.

RALPH (*referring to the call being reversed on the TV screen*): I knew it!

COMMENTATOR: Lucky break for Ralph on that one. This would be a great time to call a time out and get things sorted out down there. There's definitely something wrong with the communication.

(JEANNE *looks away and closes her eyes.*)

JEANNE: Oh, God.

COMMENTATOR: She appears to be looking to the sidelines for some help.

JEANNE: Is that what this is about?

RALPH: Is that what what is about?

JEANNE: Is this about my father living with us?

COMMENTATOR: It appeared as if they were signaling a time out on the sideline, but she shook it off and lines up in the shotgun.

RALPH: No. It's about you bugging me while I'm trying to watch my football game.

JEANNE: Bugging you? *(Sarcastic)* Oh, I'm sorry!

COMMENTATOR: She takes the snap . . .

RALPH *(to the television):* Here they come. They're reading blitz.

JEANNE: I had you confused with someone that should care.

COMMENTATOR: Jeanne throws a lateral to Ralph and he's slammed in the backfield.

(RALPH *stands and begins to pace.*)

RALPH: I knew it. Blitz. *(Takes a drink, speaks to* JEANNE*)* Talk to Joe at work about it. He seems to care enough.

(REFEREE *blows a whistle and throws a flag.*)

REFEREE: Unsportsmanlike conduct. 15-yard penalty. Third down.

COMMENTATOR: Ouch. That's about a 25-yard loss on that play alone. These two are definitely headed in the wrong direction. Someone needs to run down there and tell them their goal is the other direction.

RALPH *(to the television):* Why are these guys going without a huddle? They're lousy with the two minute drill. There's not even two minutes. It's just the beginning of the game. *(Shouting)* You got time! *(Standing now and holding his hands to his head.)* What are they thinking? Call a time out!

COMMENTATOR: Jeanne will have to air it out now. She takes the snap . . .

JEANNE: You're right. Joe would listen. Hey, maybe you could talk to him about keeping a job?

(REFEREE *blows a whistle and throws a flag.*)

REFEREE: Holding! Five yards.

RALPH: OK. That's it! What do you want from me?

JEANNE: I wanted two minutes and you couldn't give me that. You're useless.

(REFEREE *blows a whistle and throws a flag.*)

REFEREE: Unnecessary roughness! Five yards.

COMMENTATOR: They'll have to kick the ball away now after digging themselves into a deep hole.

RALPH: You just nag all the time. You sound just like your mother.

(REFEREE *blows a whistle and throws a flag.*)

REFEREE: Holding! Five yards.

JEANNE: That's because you never do anything around here except watch television and drink anymore; just like your no-good, good-for-nothing father.

(The REFEREE blows the whistle. But instead of throwing a flag down, he takes the flag(s) and throws them up into the air.)

REFEREE: That's it. I'm out of here. You're on your own. (Shakes his head and exits.)

COMMENTATOR: Here comes the kicking team onto the field.

(JEANNE throws her hands up in the air in surrender.)

JEANNE: That's it.

(She sits down on a chair or the end of the couch and puts her hands in her head.)

RALPH (to the television): What are you doing?

COMMENTATOR: Jeanne is waving off the punt team and is lining up to take the snap. This is crazy.

JEANNE: We need help, Ralph. We need to talk to the pastor or somebody.

COMMENTATOR: It looks like a Hail Mary.

RALPH (to the television): They are throwing it away?

COMMENTATOR: She steps back to throw . . .

RALPH (frantic, yelling at the television): Get rid of it. Get rid of it!

JEANNE: Can you even hear me?

COMMENTATOR: Jeanne is in her own end zone. There's no one downfield. Nothing is open.

RALPH (to the television): Don't just stand there! Run! Get out of there!

JEANNE: I'm leaving.

COMMENTATOR: Oh no! She's sacked hard.

RALPH (to the television): I can't believe it. What were you thinking?

COMMENTATOR: Oh! That was ugly. She was all alone back there and got crushed by a swarm of defensive players.

(JEANNE gets up slowly.)

RALPH (to the television): Good riddance, ya bum! Bring in a back-up.

COMMENTATOR: Jeanne gets up slowly. She's definitely hurt. I don't think she'll be back.

RALPH: What a good-fer-nothin bum!

(JEANNE exits. RALPH is oblivious to what has transpired.)

RALPH: Hey, honey! If you're going out, can get me another six-pack? I'm going to need it.

*(A door slams shut.)*

RALPH: Jeanne?

COMMENTATOR: And that's just the beginning of the game, folks, and already the Hiltibilteys are down by two.

*Blackout*

# The Red Zone

**Running Time**: 3 minutes

**Themes:** Christmas memories, Gift buying, Joy

**Scripture Reference:** Luke 2:12

**Synopsis:** Gift giving can be tough; especially for those you love the most. It's like being in an infamous red zone in football, where scoring gets harder the closer you get to the goal. In this sketch a father tries to give his grown son some pointers while they play Yahtzee.

**Cast:**
> DAD—Sports fan (Steelers, of course), 50+; an emotionally-invested father. He's a Pittsburgh kind of guy; blue collar and hard working; family oriented, but not necessarily too touchy-feely.
> BEN—Level-headed, 20+ son that didn't get all the fanatical Steelers or other sports-related genes.

**Props:**
> Yahtzee game pieces
> Pencil
> Scoring tablets

**Setting:** Kitchen table

*(BEN and DAD are sitting at the kitchen table playing Yahtzee. DAD takes the first roll of the dice. They need to continue rolling the dice and playing the game as the dialogue moves forward.)*

DAD: You are going *down.*

BEN: Dad, why are you so competitive?

DAD: Oh, and you're not?

BEN: Yeah, at games that actually require skill.

DAD: And Yahtzee doesn't require skill?

BEN: It's just rolling dice. How much skill is that?

DAD: It's playing the dice as they roll that makes it exciting. It's a game of probability and statistics.

BEN: It's luck.

DAD: It's life. There's a strategy.

BEN: OK. You're definitely over the top.

DAD: I'll show you.

(DAD *takes the dice out and mocks a roll by turning up four sixes.*)

DAD: Four sixes. Where do you put them? Top or bottom?

BEN: I . . . Four of a kind, I guess.

DAD: You guess? Tactical error, you see? Always fill in the top first because it's a 35 point bonus. You can't get that with four sixes on the bottom, right?

Ben: O . . . K . . .

(*He rearranges the dice to make another display.*)

DAD: Two, three, four, five, and five on the first roll. What are you going to do?

BEN: Uh, I go for the fives.

DAD: This is why you went to college to be a journalist instead of a rocket scientist. You roll for the large straight. One dice to get two numbers. Your chances to get a large straight just increased. And don't forget that a large straight is only ten points less than a Yahtzee.

BEN: You are scaring me.

DAD: It's a life lesson. When life gives you lemons, make lemonade. So roll.

(*They begin to play.* BEN *goes first. Remember the "rolls" need to correspond to specific lines that should be apparent by the dialogue.*)

BEN: I need to get Beth a Christmas gift.

DAD: Exactly what I'm talking about.

BEN: Beth's Christmas present?

DAD: No, no. You rolled a pair of twos and you pick up and go for your twos?

BEN: What's wrong with that?

DAD: You're not thinking! Take the six and go for your sixes. Go for high points early in the game. If you keep the twos, go for a full house. Your ones and twos on top . . . they're throw away if you need them later. (*Points to his head*) Strategy. (*Pause*) So, what are you thinking about getting her?

BEN: She was looking at some steak knives . . .

DAD: Yeah, good idea. She'll throw them at you. Trust me. We should have had this conversation a long time ago.

BEN: What conversation?

DAD: The conversation about the Red Zone. See? So, I'll take my twos here and I'm only down a couple points. I can make that up in one roll.

BEN: The Red Zone? You mean 20 yards to the goal line in football?

DAD: That's it. It's the hardest place to score because you have less field to work with. In relationships, you have only a small window of opportunity to get the gift buying wrong.

BEN: How long is that?

DAD: First five years! After that you're in the Red Zone of gift buying. Yahtzee is the same thing: It gets harder as the game goes on.

BEN: Only you could make a sports analogy out of buying a Christmas gift.

DAD *(laughing):* On our sixth Christmas together, I got your mom a scrapbook kit.

BEN: What was wrong with that?

DAD: That's what I thought. She had been talking about organizing her pictures for a year. I thought it would help. But in her mind, I was just badgering her.

BEN: I was thinking about something for the bedroom.

DAD: That's a fumble in the Red Zone. Nothing for the house and definitely no appliances. (BEN *has obviously wasted a roll.)* Now would be a good time to take your chance.

BEN: On what?

DAD: On the score card.

BEN: Oh. *(Pause)* So what happened with the scrapbook?

DAD: Fortunately, I recovered to save the day. I had bought this little knickknack; an afterthought really. It was a wooden carving of a woman sitting on a chair and holding a baby . . .

BEN: The one that Mom keeps on her dresser? (DAD *nods. Pause.)* What year was that?

DAD: Christmas 1983.

BEN *(thinking):* About nine months before I was born.

DAD *(rolling):* Yahtzee. That was big. That Christmas we had the best Christmas ever; our first Christmas as a family.

(BEN *rolls. He picks up three dice and leaves two "twos" on the table . . .)*

DAD: Your twos? You already used your twos.

BEN: I'm going for a full house.

(DAD *looks at* BEN'S *scorecard.)*

DAD: You already have your full house.

BEN: I want a full house of my own.

(DAD *pauses.)*

BEN: I think I'm getting Beth a crib for the bedroom; a baby crib.

(DAD *slowly smiles.)*

BEN: Would that work in the Red Zone?

DAD: Yeah. That's a perfect gift.

(DAD *stands up and hugs his son.)*

DAD: A perfect gift. Let's go tell your mom. *(They exit.)*

# Second Chances

**Running Time:** 2 minutes

**Themes:** Salvation, Gift-giving, Regret

**Scripture Reference:** Romans 6:23

**Synopsis:** What's the greatest gift anyone's ever given you at Christmas? What about three seconds? What would you do with it and how would you spend it? This sketch is a powerful reading by three players about the greatest gift of all.

**Cast:**
SPEAKER 1—Female
SPEAKER 2—Male
SPEAKER 3—Male
Characters are non-descript. With minor variations on the short vignettes in the center of the script, the cast can be changed to accommodate three players of either gender.

**Props:**
A decorative Christmas bag
A decorative Christmas box
A fairly ornate small bottle (such as a perfume bottle)

**Setting:** Scene can be played in any space

**Production Note:** This piece is structured for three people, however, it also works very well using an ensemble cast and working with staged pictures and some movement. Suitable for choirs too.

SPEAKER 1: Three kings

SPEAKER 2: Bearing gifts

SPEAKER 3: From afar.

SPEAKER 1: Melchior

SPEAKER 2: Balthazar

SPEAKER 3: Gaspar

SPEAKER 1: They were astrologers.

SPEAKER 2: They were wise men

SPEAKER 3: They came from the East

SPEAKER 1: Bearing the gift of gold—to identify Jesus as a king.

SPEAKER 2: Bearing the gift of frankincense—to identify Jesus as priest.

25

SPEAKER 3: Bearing the gift of myrrh—to identify Jesus as Savior.

ALL: Three kings bearing gifts.

*(Pause)*

SPEAKER 1: We are not kings.

SPEAKER 2: We are not wise men.

SPEAKER 3: We are not from so far away.

ALL: But we come bearing gifts.

SPEAKER 1 *(presents a bottle):* One second.

SPEAKER 2 *(presents a box):* One second.

SPEAKER 3 *(presents a bag):* One second.

ALL: What would you do with three seconds?

*(Pause)*

SPEAKER 1: I would have said, "yes."

SPEAKER 2: I would have said, "no."

SPEAKER 3: I wouldn't have said anything at all.

SPEAKER 1: I would have stopped.

SPEAKER 2: I would have never started.

SPEAKER 3: I would have kept on going.

SPEAKER 1: I would have never opened that door.

SPEAKER 2: I would have never gotten into that car.

SPEAKER 3: I would have never turned my back.

SPEAKER 1: If you could spend a second to relive one moment that could change your life, what would that be worth to you?

SPEAKER 2: How much would you pay for that?

SPEAKER 3: What's the value of . . .

ALL: Second chances?

*(Pause)*

SPEAKER 1: It was a split second. My dad and I were cutting brush and this log snapped and hit him on the side of the head throwing him off the ground and slamming him against this rock. He never knew what hit him.

SPEAKER 2: It was the heat of the moment. He just pushed the wrong button and I said some things . . . terrible things. I guess it was the straw that broke the camel's back. I don't know where he went and I haven't seen him since. I would do anything for one more chance.

SPEAKER 3: I remember the moment I started smoking. I was so sick. You would have thought I would have learned my lesson from that. But my friends were all doing it and I guess I was trying to fit in. I don't know. Forty years later I have lung cancer. I shouldn't be surprised, right? It's not like I didn't know the risk. I just wish I never would have started.

*(Pause)*

SPEAKER 1: The mistake most people would make

SPEAKER 2: . . . is to waste their time trying to change the past

SPEAKER 3: . . . instead of investing it in the future.

SPEAKER 1: Take the gift of three seconds

SPEAKER 2: And make it . . .

SPEAKER 3: An eternity.

ALL: That's the gift of God at Christmas.

SPEAKER 1: Kairos became Chronos.

SPEAKER 2: Infinity became a moment.

SPEAKER 3: Time stops.

SPEAKER 1: The gift of God is eternal life in Christ Jesus,

SPEAKER 2: So that if you confess with your mouth that Jesus is Lord,

SPEAKER 3: And believe in your heart God raised Him from the dead,

ALL: You will be saved.

SPEAKER 3: And Chronos becomes Kairos,

SPEAKER 2: And a moment becomes infinity,

SPEAKER 1: And time begins again.

ALL: All in about three seconds.

SPEAKER 1: One. Confess with your mouth.

SPEAKER 2: Two. Believe in your heart.

SPEAKER 3: Three. And you will be saved.

ALL: Three seconds.

# Black Friday

**Running Time:** 4 minutes

**Themes:** Depression, Perspective, our God is in the midst of *all* our circumstances

**Scripture Reference:** Psalms 71:20

**Synopsis:** Ever get those letters at Christmas that bring glad tidings from loved ones only to make you think your life is a wreck? This sketch reminds us that regardless of our situation, we all have much to be thankful for.

**Cast:**
MAN—Mid 40s, out of work but *in* a mid-life crisis. He's at home taking care of the housework while his wife is working.

**Props:**
Basket of laundry
Bottle of Fresh Start laundry detergent
Mail to include bills and letters

*(Note: The envelope that has the words "Victory Report" on it, does not have to be an actual prop. It can be a generic sales letter from any commercial company trying to sell you something. The audience will not be able to read what's on the envelope.)*

**Setting:** A table and one chair at the end of the table. It's a folding table in a laundry room.

*(MAN enters the stage. He is carrying laundry in a basket with a stack of mail lying on top of the clothes. There are also a few clothespins and a bottle of Fresh Start in the basket. He begins sorting through the mail until he spots the "letter.")*

MAN: Oh no, the annual bliss report from the Walkers.

*(He examines the outside of the letter thoughtfully.)*

Do I *really* want to know how exciting their year was . . . *again*; the success stories about their five straight-A children and trips to exotic places all over the world. I'll bet they had these done and in the mail before their Thanksgiving trip to Vail this year.

*(He tosses the letter onto the table. He notices the next letter in the pile. It is a newsletter from a large, prestigious ministry.)*

Oh, now this should cheer me up! "Victory Report." *(Sneers)* Could they just print that in bigger red letters?

*(He pulls the stapled newsletter open. His tone is very sarcastic.)*

28

Ah, isn't that sweet? There's Brother Ken Riggleman walking the dog and smiling at his beautiful, Barbie-doll wife with her recently completed eye tucks. And there's his perfect little son, Jimmy, and his perfect little sister, Della. Pink ruffles . . . Isn't that . . .

*(He rips up the letter.)*

Precious.

*(He sings this line to the tune of* Jingle Bells.*)*

Victory, victory, Vic'try all the way. *(He sighs.)* You know just *once*, I'd like Brother Ken to send out a *reality report*.

*(He imagines reading from another letter.)*

Greetings Prayer Warriors! This is Commander Ken and G-I'm Barbie. We want you to know the truth for once! We're tired of fighting evil. We're not even winning the battles in our lives. Our marriage stinks and our kids are out of control. Actually, we're thinking about giving up the ministry and taking a break. We just can't find the will to take one more hill for Jesus. So, I think we're going to pull out and try and work through this mess. Until then, you're on your own. Oh, and have a great Christmas.

*(He puts the letter down on the table.)*

Am I the only one on the planet whose world is falling apart?

*(This next section of script is played out using the pile of laundry. He speaks to it as if he's the CEO of a company firing one of the employees. He first moves to the basket of laundry and sets it down in front of him.)*

Company's in a heap of trouble, son!

*(He pulls out the bottle of Fresh Start laundry detergent just underneath the pile.)*

What we need around here is a "Fresh Start."

*(He puts down the bottle, takes one of the shirts and shakes it out in front of him.)*

So we're shaking things up around here and . . .

*(He holds the shirt out in front of him and then lays it out on the table.)*

I'm going to lay it out for you. You're all washed up.

*(He pulls out a couple of clothespins from the pile of laundry and starts to snap them at the shirt on the table.)*

We're going to hang you out to dry.

*(He attaches the clothespin to the shirt and holds up the clothespin in front of him with the shirt dangling off the pin.)*

Ha! How does it feel, you old rag?

*(He catches himself and throws the shirt and pin back onto the pile.)*

I'm talking to laundry! What's the matter with me?

*(He puts his head into his hands and pauses. As he gathers up the mail, he notices the catalog on top of the pile. He lets out a "Hmmmph" and picks it up to look at it momentarily.)*

Right! This is just what we need. "For the family who has it all . . . limited edition, collector's series, pewter nativity set." Shepherds, wise men, cows, sheep, donkeys . . . Look at that! No baby in the manger. Guess that comes extra.

*(He sits down and looks at the magazine cover. Then he looks around the room.)*

Now that *would* be some good news. Please tell me that You're not in that pewter manger, Lord. I need to know that You're not in that kind of place; a place that's only for a few who have their acts together. I need You to be real in my world. Real life; like a guy out of work and playing Mr. Mom while his wife has to go to work to pay the bills and feed the family.

*(He reaches for the pile of mail again and starts pulling envelopes out of the stack.)*

Real, like electric bills, house payments, credit card bills, bills . . .

*(He shakes the stack of envelopes above his head.)*

This is my reality, Lord. I've gotten so cynical. One day after Thanksgiving and I'm thankless again. Maybe that's why they call it "Black Friday". I want to see You in the manger with the dirt, and the stink, and the pain, and the tears. That's what it's like down here. Please, please . . . I need You to come into this manger and bring a little light . . . please.

*(He sighs again and reaches over to the "bliss letter" from the Walkers. He opens it and begins to read.)*

"Dear friends: This is not going to be like most of the annual letters of good cheer you receive from so many. Dave began having severe headaches in August. When they began to interfere with his work schedule, he went to have it checked out. The prognosis is not good. Dave has a brain tumor that seems to be enlarging slowing but surely. Needless to say, it has been a most difficult time for us and we desperately need your prayers of support. But through it all, we have sensed the presence of God in a new and different way . . ."

*(He pauses and sets the letter down next to him.)*

Forgive me, Lord. Please forgive me.

*(He kneels next to his chair and begins to pray.)*

**Note:** Another rendition of this script to be performed by a woman, entitled "Victory Report," is available in the sketch collection *Body, Mind and Spirit*, copyright © 1999 by Lillenas Publishing Company. (www.lillenas.com)

# Simeon

**Running Time:** 3-4 minutes

**Themes:** Perseverance, Patience, Blessing, Christmas

**Scripture Reference:** Luke 2:25-35

**Synopsis:** Simeon's promise is fulfilled as he finally sees the Messiah. An optional ending provides suggested music to go with the monologue.

**Cast:**

SIMEON—Male, 60+

**Production Note:** This piece includes an optional ending with music.

*(SIMEON is feeding the pigeons in the courtyard of the temple. This is something he does daily as he goes out into the day to examine the courtyard.)*

SIMEON: Here pidgy, pidgy. Here pidgy . . . come and get something to eat. Dometrius, is that you? Come here my feathered, weathered friend. You look tired . . . and old. I suppose it happens if you live long enough. I used to think old was always 15 years older than I was. But, now . . . So what brings you back this day of days? Have you come to rest? Hmmmph. No rest for you here my friend. Do you see that box over there?

*(He points offstage.)*

The trumpet chest third from the left? It might as well be a coffin for you, but to us it is a collection box for a burnt offering. Then a priest will count out the coins, take you and a couple of your friends around the neck and . . .

*(SIMEON pantomimes a slicing motion on his neck.)*

Look now into the Court of the Priests and see the blood of your brothers rise up as an offering unto the Lord. Sacrifices . . . grisly business.

*(He prays.)*

"But he who avenges blood, he doesn't ignore the cry of those afflicted."

Ah, nowhere is safe, Dometrius. Out there are soldiers, horses, spears, armor. Out there, Rome rules with an iron grip and they punish resistance ruthlessly. We can only watch as they confiscate our homes, violate our women, and demoralize our nation. Be glad you're a bird and not a Jew. What it is like? Oy. I can describe to you in three words . . . Suff-er-ing. We are God's chosen. Hmmmph. Sometimes, I wish He would choose someone else.

*(SIMEON prays.)*

"Hear our just cause, O Lord." "God, heed my cry." "Give ear to my prayer, which is not from deceitful lips. Let Your judgment come forth from Your presence. Let Your eyes look with equity." The Psalms, Dometrius. We shall pray down our enemies with the Psalms. I will teach them to you so that you can defeat your foes, also. What news do you bring from far away places? Have you seen the star that shines over Bethlehem? It first appeared 41 days ago. Don't look surprised. Everyone pays something. I pay attention. What else am I to do, eh? I'm surprised you haven't seen it at night. Perhaps you can't see at night? It is a sign, Dometrius. "Yet you, oh Bethlehem, though you be small among the nations, yet shall you be the birthplace of a King." Birthplace of a King, Dometrius. And I have heard talk, villagers, merchants, travelers, they speak of shepherds who tell of angels announcing the birth of the King—a Savior. Perhaps, the long awaited, Messiah? Shhhh. But Dometrius, this is the thing . . . the shepherds were led to Bethlehem by the angels, to a baby born in a manger. A baby? Perhaps a baby-King? *(Pause)* So, do you see it now? Ah foolish bird. It's the Law of Moses. A woman who gives birth to a child is unclean for 40 days of her impurity. But after this period she must offer up a lamb as a burnt offering and—a turtledove or *pigeon*—we'll pray that it is a turtledove, Dometrius . . . as a sin offering. We shouldn't talk of such things, huh? But, it *could* be today. A woman, carrying a child, enters the Temple area through the North side, the Gate of the Women, and then heads East, to the area of the colonnades to the trumpet chest to deposit her offering. Hmm?

Come here old bird. We will wait together. Rest awhile.

**Ending #1:**

*(Something seems to leap in* SIMEON'S *spirit and he looks up from feeding the pigeon. Perhaps it is the sound of a child crying. He sees Mary and Joseph enter the temple area with the baby in their arms. He slowly rises as he speaks. Note: Mary, Joseph and the baby do not need to be real characters acting out this part.* SIMEON *can pantomime his motions 'as if' they were visible to the audience.)*

O God the procession of my God and King comes into the sanctuary.

A woman . . . and her husband with a Child, newly born—climbing the steps . . . 10, 11, 12 . . . through the Gate of the Women on the North Side . . . They travel . . . East . . . towards the treasury and . . . third box on the left.

*(He moves towards them. He "hands" the pigeon to Joseph. He speaks to Mary as he holds out his arms.)*

Please, may I?

*(He takes the 'child' and looks upon it. He speaks to Mary and Joseph but does not take his eyes off the 'child' until he mentions that sword that will pierce Mary's soul.)*

This Child is destined to cause the falling and rising of many in Israel, and to be a sign that will be spoken against, so that the thoughts of many hearts will be revealed. And a sword will pierce your own soul too.

*(He speaks to Joseph.)*

Take the pigeon and give him to the priest. Tell him Simeon says, "He is an offering without blemish to cover your sins . . .

(SIMEON *looks at the child.*)

. . . and the sins of the world.

(SIMEON *returns the child to Mary and they depart.*)

Now Lord, dismiss your servant in peace.

(*Lights fade as he exits.*)


## Optional Ending #2:

(SIMEON *sings verse one of the song,* Welcome to Our World)

(*Then* SIMEON *stops and looks up. He sees the woman carrying a baby just as he has always visualized it in his dreams and in his mind. He slowly rises up from where he sits to feed the pigeon.* SIMEON *speaks during verse two of the song. He makes a commentary on their movements as if he knows where they are going before they get there saying:*)

O God the procession of my God and King comes into the sanctuary.
A woman and her husband with a Child, newly born—climbing the steps . . . 10, 11, 12 . . . through the Gate of the Women on the North Side . . . They travel . . . East . . . towards the treasury and . . . third box on the left.

(*He moves towards them. He "hands" the pigeon to Joseph. He says to Mary:*)

Please, may I?

(SIMEON *sings verse three.*)

(*Then* SIMEON *says to Mary during verse four of the song:*)

This Child is destined to cause the falling and rising of many in Israel, and to be a sign that will be spoken against, so that the thoughts of many hearts will be revealed. And a sword will pierce Your own soul too.

(SIMEON *sings the last verse.*)

(*Then* SIMEON *says to Joseph:*)

Take the pigeon and give him to the priest.
Tell him Simeon says, "He is an offering without blemish to cover your sins (SIMEON *looks at the child.*) . . . and the sins of the world.

(SIMEON *returns the child to Mary and they depart.*)

Now Lord, dismiss Your servant in peace.

(*He exits as lights fade.*)

# A Carpenter's Rule

**Running Time:** 3-4 minutes

**Themes:** Trust, God's sovereignty, Christmas, Advent

**Scripture:** Matthew 1:18-25

**Synopsis:** A piece that explores the deep feelings Joseph has after hearing news that Mary is with child.

**Cast:**
> JOSEPH—Male, mid-20s, traditional Bible character
> GABRIEL—Male/Female, 20+

*(JOSEPH enters. He seems dazed and confused, and aimlessly wanders onto the scene toward his workbench where he begins to handle some wooden pieces laying near his work bench. He eventually picks up a plane and starts to run it along the grain of the wood. It is a mindless action that he does routinely. He is obviously distraught and distracted. Eventually his emotions turn to anger and he begins to run the plane into the wood until it falls from his hands and on to the floor. He nearly collapses onto the workbench, but holds himself over it as if he would rather vomit.)*

JOSEPH: Think, Joseph. Think straight.

*(He clutches his hands to his head.)*
> I must pray.

*(He finds his way to the end of the work bench. He stands there momentarily but cannot bend his knees.)*
> If I close my eyes, I will only see her face and . . . hear her voice.

*(He slowly closes his eyes.)*
> "I . . . am . . . with . . . child."

*(He puts his hands over his ears as if to drown out his own voice.)*
> No! No! It cannot be. Think, Joseph. Why would she say she was with child? Did I move too quickly? Perhaps not quickly enough. I should have taken her when I had the chance.

*(He mocks the voices of those who counseled him in this regard.)*
> "Do the honorable thing, Joseph." "Be patient, Joseph." "It's her parent's wishes, Joseph." Stand back and wait while someone else takes the girl I've waited for all my life.
>
> Think, Joseph. Perhaps I misunderstood her. Maybe she said she was *with a* child. Maybe she was with Rachel or Sarah. *(He laughs.)* She loves to play with the children. She's no more than a child herself. Sweet little Mary. . . so young. So . . .

(*He moves toward the wall and runs his hands over the 'stone wall.'*)

I've just been working so hard trying to get this place ready in time for the wedding; too hard. (*Pause*) It's too hard . . .

(*He slumps down against the wall.*)

How could it be? She said she has not known another man. She said she loves me and then . . . she blames God.

(*He rises up as he considers the implication of Mary's admission.*)

She lies . . . she blasphemes . . . and her sin is . . . adultery, the penalty for which is *death.*

(*He has picked up a gavel or hammer nearby and strikes a blow to the workhorse as if he has brought the sentence down upon her himself in judgment.*)

*Death!* She must be stoned in the town square according to the Law . . . she . . .

(*He drops the hammer out of his hand and steps away from the workhorse. He is frightened by his own response.*)

What am I saying? I love her.

(*He falls to his knees.*)

Her lips could never speak a lie. A dreamer, yes . . . but a liar . . . never. Think, Joseph. I must pray.

(*As he closes his eyes to pray, he realizes he is praying to a God who has become his rival. He opens his eyes and looks at his hands.*)

Pray?

(*The notion strikes him as absurd. He stands and looks up to confront his Adversary.*)

How shall I pray to the One who is the victor? How shall I pray to the One who stole my fiancé from me? Shall I beg for . . . mercy? (*He laughs.*) Mercy? Shall I ask for mercy from Him who has shown none? You could have had anyone. You're the All-powerful; the Almighty. Is this the way You show Your strength? Do You take what doesn't belong to You? You took my love from me! (*Pause. He considers the situation and the unusual position in which he finds himself.*) But I will have the last say. (*He laughs.*) What a strange twist of fate. Your life is now in my hands. Speak to me. Show yourself! Fight me for the right to her hand. I would rather die than be without her. *Say something!*

(*Pause*)

Silence?

(*Pause*)

Quiet? Is that it?

(*His anger subsides and his energy leaks from him like air in a balloon. He is deflated and defeated.*)

Think, Joseph. I must be rational. I must do what is best for Mary. Yes. I could go quietly to the elders and nullify my engagement to marry her on the terms of desertion. No one would suspect as long as she stays in Jerusalem. It will save her from scandal. *(Resolved)* I'll write to her in the morning and tell her I don't ever want to see her again. *(Pause)* It couldn't be any worse than the lie she told me.

I can't think anymore. I can't . . .

*(JOSEPH lies down on the floor in front of the work bench. He is soon asleep.)*

*(Note: The script can end here or another character, GABRIEL, can be added. GABRIEL enters.)*

GABRIEL: Wake up, Joseph.

*(JOSEPH begins to stir as if coming out of deep sleep. He sits up and stretches and then sees GABRIEL. He grabs hold of the hammer nearby and moves to confront the angel.)*

JOSEPH: Wh . . . whh . . . who are you? Wh . . . what do you wa . . . want here?

*(GABRIEL stretches out his/her hand toward the hammer. As he/she lowers his/her hand, JOSEPH's arm is lowered against his will and the hammer falls to the floor. JOSEPH grabs his hand and cradles it as it begins to shake.)*

GABRIEL: Joseph, son of David, don't hesitate to take Mary as your wife. For the Child within her has been conceived by the Holy Spirit just as she has told you. And she will have a Son and you shall call His name "Jesus," meaning "Savior." This shall fulfill the message of the prophets, who said, "Behold! A virgin shall conceive a child! She shall give birth to a son and he shall be called, 'Emmanuel' which means, 'God with us.'"

*(JOSEPH closes his eyes as GABRIEL steps backwards several steps before turning and exiting.)*

JOSEPH: The virgin will be with child and she will give birth to a son and he shall be called . . . *(he opens his eyes)* Emmanuel.

*(JOSEPH falls to his knees. The realization that the time of the Promised One is upon them is dawning on him as he speaks the scripture and remembers the angel's words.)*

How could this be? Jahveh, I am just a carpenter of no means. And Mary is just a girl of 14 . . . almost 15. She is just a child herself. There are others better able. Please! Please, I beg you; not Mary . . . not me . . . and not now!

*(JOSEPH exits crying out Mary's name.)*

# Mary's Moment

**Running Time:** 3 minutes

**Theme:** Trust, Advent, Christmas

**Scripture:** Luke 1:26-38

**Synopsis:** A short piece that captures Mary in the moment of being told she is to be the mother of the Son of God.

**Cast:**
> MARY—Female, age 15+, playful, innocent, and very much in love, traditional biblical character.

**Production Notes:** This monologue also plays in a purely historical setting, recreating the moment of the Annunciation. This piece also plays well with musical (instrumental) underscore.

*(The scene is a path outside the town of Nazareth. A young woman (15-20) enters the stage carrying a basket filled with a load of clean laundry. She is coming back from doing her washing at a nearby river. She is singing merrily and stepping lightly. She stops and drops her load, then spins with her arms open wide. She is giddy with joy. Spying her beloved's jacket in the pile of clothes, she bends down and picks it up, holding it in front of her at the collar as if it were a man standing there.)*

MARY: Well Joseph, how did you like my song?

*(She pauses and acts dismayed.)*
> Oh! You thought I sounded like a cricket, did you? Well, how would you like it if this cricket took your nice clean clothes and threw them along the path.

*(She drops the jacket and picks a shirt out of the basket and acts as though she is going to throw it away. She speaks coyly, as if he is standing there.)*
> Now, you must say something nice, to make up for your unkind remark! *(Pause)* Hmmm? You *love* me?

*(She acts surprised.)*
> And you want to marry me?

*(She plays coy with him as she puts the shirt back in the basket.)*
> Well, first I must see how good you are at dancing, because I could never marry someone who can't dance.

*(She takes the jacket by the arms and begins singing as she dances openly and freely with the jacket in her arms. As she spins around, she stops suddenly as if seeing someone unexpected or a stranger. Make sure that the basket is between her and the angel during their conversation.)*

Oh, hello?

*(She is taken back by the stranger's sudden appearance.)*
Who are you? How did you know my name? I don't think I've ever seen you on this path before. Are you new to the town?

*(Pause. She is startled and then shocked by the stranger's response.)*
You are lying, because you say that I shall have a child. But, that is not possible. *(Shyly)* I am a virgin. Now, if you will please let me go my way.

*(As she speaks again, she turns and kneels to put the jacket in the basket and then lifts the basket up between herself and the stranger. She is going to try to move past him but as she turns and faces him, the stranger speaks again. Pause. She stops as if frozen. After a moment of pause, she drops the basket abruptly.)*
The Messiah?

*(Pause. She drops to the ground as if her knees give way. She makes no sound but for a gasp. She can not lift her face to the stranger.)*
I am the Lord's servant. May it be done to me as you have said.

*(Pause. Finally, as if awakened from a dream, she lifts her face slowly, but whoever was speaking to her is gone. She looks around momentarily and then back at the basket in front of her. She picks it up and begins to stand with it, but drops it again.)*
It is too heavy a load to carry.

*(She looks down at the basket.)*
I must do the wash.

*(She kneels next to the basket.)*
But the clothes are clean. Yes, I cleaned them myself at the river, Father. I don't know how they got dirty.

*(Pause. She looks up.)*
I don't know how . . .

*(She stops abruptly and puts her hand over her mouth. She looks down at the basket again and picks up the jacket she used in the beginning of the scene. She holds it in front of her as she stands again.)*
Joseph! You said you loved me. You said you would marry me. Joseph?

*(She drops the jacket and runs offstage leaving the basket behind her.)*

# The Shepherd

**Running Time:** 3-4 minutes

**Themes:** Forgiveness, Love, Sacrifice, Christmas, Advent

**Scripture:** Luke 2:8-17

**Synopsis:** A young shepherd shares the news of the baby Messiah with his estranged wife expressing how God can change his life and restore their relationship.

**Cast:**

> SHEPHERD—Male, age 18+

*(The SHEPHERD is an anachronistic character played as a '90s slacker. He is wearing a black beanie cap and an Army fatigue jacket. All references to Sarah are pantomimed or played as if she were in the scene, seated on a chair CS. The SHEPHERD enters on a dead run. He spots "Sarah" sitting in a chair or standing by a window and quickly moves toward her.)*

SHEPHERD: *Sarah! Sarah!* Oh Sarah, there you are! Look, you're not going to believe what just happened to me! OK, me and the boys, right, we were sit'n up in the fields, you know, like we always do, just watch'n your daddy's stinkin' sheep. I hate those stupid sheep. I mean . . .

*(He is beyond himself with excitement, but he is trying to be very careful of how he speaks to Sarah. There should be the appearance of an awkward tension in their relationship.)*

> The sheep stink, not your daddy, right? Right! Anyway, it was me and the boys; uh,Tommy, Charlie, Doogy, Big John, Little John, Ray Ray, and me, right, just sittin' there. Then, all of a sudden, there was this stinkin' light all around us, and this big boomin' thunder sound right? Then I look up in the sky and see this big ole honk'n angel, man. And he was all like . . .

*(He flaps his hands at his side, shoulder high, like little wings, and speaks in a "ghost-like" voice. He assumes this position every time he speaks as the angel.)*

> "Don't be afraid."

*(As you play both the angel and the SHEPHERD in this short section, make sure that you look up towards the angel when you are the SHEPHERD and down towards the stage when you are the angel.)*

> I was like, "Well, that ain't workin' very well!" Anyway the angel keeps on talkin', right? "I've got some really, really, good news for you, which will make everybody really, really happy!" I was like, "OK, I'm here for the good news and then I'm history, you know?" Then this angel starts saying, "This very day in the city of Bethlehem, the Messiah has come." I'm think'n, "Whoa, that's good news. We've been waitin' around a long time to hear that, huh?" Oh, and

this is the best part right, this angel says, "You will know who He is because you will find Him dressed in baby clothes . . ."

*(The* SHEPHERD *looks puzzled for a beat.)*

Yeah, right! The Messiah in baby clothes? *(The* SHEPHERD *laughs)* That's what I was think'n, but it wasn't like that at all, man! Oh, OK, right, this is the best part, man. Then with the big honkin' angel . . . *(He looks up into the air around him.)* . . . there's all these *little* honkin' angels and they're all . . . (SHEPHERD *pantomimes playing an instrument like a horn.)* Honkin'! Yeah, they are gettin' down with these instruments, man. It was awesome.

*(*SHEPHERD *tries to dance.)*

And me and the boys was dancing!

*(*SHEPHERD *looks at Sarah.)*

Remember how we used to dance . . . together, Sarah?

*(There is an awkward or strained silence between them.)*

Anyway, after this party died down, Little John was like, "Hey, let's go find this Messiah like the angel was talkin' about." So we all got into Ray Ray's truck and headed out for Bethlehem. Eventually, man, we found this couple, right, in this barn! Whoowee, man! There were stinkin' animals all over the place. I can't get away from the smell, ya know?

*(He pinches his nose.)*

But, they had this cute little baby, man, and he's lying in this manger. We were all around this baby making cute little baby faces at Him.

*(*SHEPHERD *pretends to look in the manger at the baby and play a little game of 'hide and seek.' He covers his eyes.)*

Where's the baby?

*(He uncovers his eyes.)*

There's the baby!

*(The* SHEPHERD *repeats this at least one more time.)*

And, like, Big John was singing this baby song, you know, *(sings)* "Mary had a little lamb." I wanted to smack him, man. I said, "You're embarrassing me." Then I start thinkin', "Hey, we need to be lookin' for the Messiah in baby clothes." All of a sudden it hits me! It's like, what if . . . So I lean into the manger to get a really good look at the baby, you know? Just about then, He opens his eyes . . . *(Pause)* And I could see all the way to eternity, Sarah. That's when I knew it Sarah! The Messiah is in baby clothes . . . because the Messiah is a *baby*! *(He yells out loud.)* The Messiah is a *baby*! God is a little baby laying down in Bethlehem in a stinkin' manger. *It's Him!* I know it! It was great! We were all high fivin' each other and cheering and hugging this couple, man! It was like serendipity, baby! I don't even know what that word means! But it has to be something like this.

*(*SHEPHERD *changes mood and tone. He becomes a little more serious and introspective.)*

I was so excited, Sarah. I mean, I had to go tell somebody, right? And I knew it had to be you. I ran all the way back up the hill from Bethlehem to get you. I had to come and take you down there because I want you to see this and well, because I started thinkin', "If God can change that much for me, then, maybe I could change for Him . . . for us. Sarah, I'm so sorry . . . I mean for everything . . . I know you've heard me say it before, but this time I can change . . .

(*About this point, Sarah abruptly gets up off the chair and leaves the room. She can't stand to listen to another promise from him of how things will be better and how this time he will change. It's an old, tired line for her and she doesn't believe him anymore. He begs her not to go.*)

Sarah, wait! Don't go, please! Sarah, I'm begging you!

(*The* SHEPHERD *falls to his knees. He is distraught and grieved. He cries as he prays.*)

God. *I can change.* If You can change that much for me, then I could be different, too! I need one more chance. Please. Please bring her back.

(*Sarah reenters the scene. She forgot her hat or other article of clothing. He is surprised, but grateful to see her. He tries to quickly compose himself.*)

Sarah? Oh yeah, you forgot your hat. (*He holds out his hand to stop her. She seems startled.*)

Sarah, please. I beg you. Go down there with me to see this thing. (*She turns to leave.*) Sarah. Look in my eyes. You'll see. I want you to know like I knew when I looked in that baby's eyes. (*pause*) I can change.

(*Pause. She agrees to go with him, walking behind him at a distance. He is so relieved that he almost begins to weep again. He speaks as if he's a schoolboy and he's not sure what to say or do next.*)

OK. We'll just go down there then.

(*He walks a half step ahead of her and on the US side so that he is facing the audience as they exit the scene to SR.*)

Oh Sarah, you're not going to believe what a cute baby He is. Well, He's not a little baby, He's more like a little God. But, He's the cutest little God I ever saw, you know? Doogy said we should call Him Jo-Jo. I said, "We ain't callin' that baby Jo-Jo. His name's Jesus. Didn't you hear His mother, man? You never listen . . ."

(*They exit as his voice fades out.*)

# The Innkeeper's Wife

**Running Time:** 3-4 minutes

**Themes:** Advent, looking for God in unexpected places, Deception

**Scripture:** Luke 2:7

**Synopsis:** A disgruntled Innkeeper's Wife expresses her disdain for letting Mary and Joseph stay near her inn.

**Cast:**

> INNKEEPER'S WIFE—Female, 35+, dutiful and responsible wife of the Innkeeper at Bethlehem. She is practical but also savvy and shrewd in the ways of business.

*(The scene takes place around an inn in Bethlehem, most likely in a waiting or registration area of the inn. The INNKEEPER'S WIFE is standing behind a counter or desk going over a list of things she needs to do for the next day. The audience becomes a customer that comes in to check on something or just relax. The three dots (. . .) represent a pause or dialogue from the client that is unheard.)*

INNKEEPER'S WIFE: All settled in? . . . Is there anything else you need? . . . Good! Why don't you have a seat? . . . I've always got time for a customer of the Bethlehem Inn. I was just going over tomorrow's breakfast menu . . . What's that? . . . Oh, yes, I love it here. It isn't always this busy, you know. Goodness knows we can use the business. The whole thing is a Godsend really. Bethlehem isn't your typical resort town, if you know what I mean. And to keep a place like this up and running . . . Well, you can understand. Who'd have ever thought Caesar would do *us* such a favor, huh?

> I always dreamed of running a place like this—quiet, little country bread and breakfast thing. James used to deal in fabrics with merchants from Greece but the riff raff in the market took advantage of him and, well, the whole thing just got ugly. Life is slower here . . . except for tonight.

*(She looks out a side window.)*

> Look at all those people. They flow through the streets like water. You have to wonder where they're from; what they're thinking; *(emphatic)* where in the world they're going to stay tonight! You were one of the smart ones to come in early for the census.

> Oh, look at that one over there. Nice jewelry, huh? I wonder where they're staying? I guess there were a *few* people from Bethlehem who actually did something with their lives. I just thought the whole lot of them turned out to be shepherds! You know, the whole thing is a great opportunity to build up clientele; meet the *right* people; make contacts.

> Our son has been on the streets all day trying to steer people our way or

other people . . . "away" . . . if you know what I mean. James is screening people at the desk . . . Oh, we get an occasional religious leader in here once in awhile. Merchants from Greece are quite common too. Oh my! Look over there. She's out to here.

*(She holds her hand out in front of her stomach as if she were pregnant.)*

She looks like she could drop that load any minute. I do feel sorry for her, I suppose. I remember when I was pregnant with my first. You couldn't have gotten me off of the bed to go anywhere, Caesar or otherwise. And he looks so young. I wonder if they're married. If they are I bet they haven't been married for long; not long enough, if you know what I mean. We've had to deal with people like that to make a go of it here. But we're moving away from that and appealing to a different crowd. Look, James is talking to them now. They're probably looking for another handout.

*(This type of thing is really a pet peeve of the* INNKEEPER'S WIFE.*)*

It really irks me. Come on James, just tell them there's no room and be on about your business . . . You probably think I'm pretty hard, don't you? Well, you learn when you're in business. It takes discretion and certain savvy to build a reputation. You can't start making exceptions. Well, would you want her in the room next to yours? Do you want to share your bathroom with her tonight? See, what I mean? If we let them in tonight, by the end of the week all the drunken, homeless, wayward con artists will be lined up outside the door waiting to get in. No, it's better for everyone this way . . . Why is James wasting time with them? We've got paying customers who need his attention. Room 21 still hasn't got their linens yet and 15 needs more oil in their lamps. Come on . . . Come on! Maybe I can help him out of this. Excuse me.

*(She steps away from the counter or desk and looks offstage towards the area where her husband is. She speaks sweetly.)*

James, dear, we need to get . . . what? Pillows and bedding? But where on earth are you . . . the stable? But, what about . . . *(Exasperated)* Yes, dear.

*(She moves back to the desk or table and speaks sarcastically.)*

Yes, dear. Oh, he'll hear about this later you can bet. Vagrants in the stable! If the town hears about this we'll be ruined. And on tonight of all nights! We better be getting something out of this is all I can say.

*(She exits in a huff.)*

# The Christmas Narrative

**Running Time:** 4 minutes *(without monologues, sketches, and suggested songs)*

**Theme:** The Christmas Story

**Scripture References:** Matthew 1:18-25, 2:1-12; Luke 2:1-20

**Synopsis:** A staged reading of the birth of Christ from portions of Matthew and Luke to be performed from within the congregation; a dynamic approach to bringing God's Word to life in the midst of the people.

**Cast:**
NARRATOR 1
NARRATOR 2
MARY
ELIZABETH
ANGEL 1
ANGEL 2
ANGEL CHOIR*
SHEPHERD
MAGI 1
MAGI 2
MAGI 3
HEROD
TEACHER 1
TEACHER 2

*The part of the Angel Choir can be read by anyone holding a script. A separate person can be assigned to read the part of the Angel Choir or this section can be read by an actually choir from their traditional space in the sanctuary.*

**Costumes:** Traditional biblical dress

**Production Notes:** This is a dramatic or staged reading, which means the script is read without set or the use of props, in this case. The "dramatic convention" is a very simple one: Assign speaking parts to persons within the congregation or assembly and tell them to stand up just prior to the delivery of their assigned parts and then to sit after their section in the story is completed. This instruction eliminates the idea of getting up and down during a section where a character has lines interspersed in dialogue. You may also instruct them to make the delivery of their line "towards" the person they are addressing in the script. In other words, Elizabeth will look at Mary when she sees her and delivers her lines. This simple dramatic convention brings the story alive in the midst of the people and provides a wonderful element of surprise. If you would like to elaborate this simple script into a longer production, I have added places where other scripts in this collection or a suggested hymn may be used. You can use some or all of these suggestions. You can also intersperse traditional or other familiar Christmas songs throughout.

Besides the basic and most fundamental delivery of this piece as a dramatic reading to include projection, enunciation, inflections, and phrasing, there are several other ideas that can enhance the dramatic element. For example:

Underscore the entire piece with instrumental music that reflects a more somber mood. I recommend *Silent Night* by Chris Rice, on his album, *The Living Room Sessions, Christmas*.

The actual narration can be a little long and tedious in parts. I have tried to make this more interesting by dividing these renderings between two Narrators. I recommend the use of contrasting voices like old and young, male and female, or cultural shifts in voice timbers and tones. Make cuts where appropriate, especially during the longer narratives.

Be sensitive to the timing, especially if you consider musical underscore. As written without adding the vignettes, the piece fits perfectly over the recommended music if you keep the pace moving. This is *not* accomplished by rushing lines, but by keeping the synapses or space between lines short and succinct, events between "scene changes".

Everyone should stand in their places, which is where they are seated in the sanctuary. That's the joy and simplicity of the piece. However, I recommend that the Narrators either walk casually around the sanctuary space as they deliver their lines or be staged right and left on the platform. I do *not* recommend voice amplification unless you are in a huge space that absolutely requires it. First of all, if you amplify one voice, you must amplify them all; otherwise your audience will have to constantly make adjustments. Secondly, this piece is dramatic because of its primitive or natural feel and the use of electronics to amplify the voice is in contrast to my intentions here. Make your players use their instrument effectively.

There is one more staging suggestion for your consideration. I like to "frame" this piece with the use of a pastor or worship leader who begins the selection by inviting the audience to turn to their Bibles and read along as he/she reads from Luke 2, beginning in verse 1. As the leader begins to read, the dramatic element "usurps" the rendering as if the words leap off the page and into the audience. The leader should not be surprised by this. Actually, I prefer that the leader continue "reading" silently as if he/she is completely unaware of what is taking place in the congregation, as if the people were being made privy to the incarnation of God's Word all over again. This continues until the very last line or so, when the leader would once again read from the text, as if never having been interrupted at all.

NARRATOR 1: In the sixth month, God sent the angel Gabriel to Nazareth, a town in Galilee, to a virgin pledged to be married to a man named Joseph. The virgin's name was Mary.

ANGEL: Greetings, you who are highly favored! The Lord is with you.

NARRATOR 2: Mary was greatly troubled at his words and wondered what kind of greeting this might be.

ANGEL: Do not be afraid, Mary, you have found favor with God. You will be with child and give birth to a son, and you are to give him the name Jesus. He will be great and will be called the Son of the Most High. The Lord God will give him the throne of his father David, and he will reign over the house of Jacob forever; his kingdom will never end.

MARY: How will this be since I am a virgin?

ANGEL: The Holy Spirit will come upon you, and the power of the Most High will overshadow you, so the holy one to be born will be called the Son of God. Even Elizabeth your relative is going to have a child in her old age, and she who was said to be barren is in her sixth month. For nothing is impossible with God.

MARY: I am the Lord's servant. May it be as you have said to me.

*(Suggested drama:* Mary's Moment*)*

NARRATOR 1: Sometime later, Mary got ready and went to a town in the hill country of Judea, where she entered Zechariah's home and greeted Elizabeth. When Elizabeth heard Mary's greeting, the baby leaped in her womb, and Elizabeth was filled with the Holy Spirit.

ELIZABETH: Blessed are you among women, and blessed is the child you will bear! But why am I so favored, that the mother of my Lord should come to me? As soon as the sound of your greeting reached my ears, the baby in my womb leaped for joy.

MARY: My soul glorifies the Lord and my spirit rejoices in God my Savior, for he has been mindful of the humble state of his servant. From now on all generations will call me blessed, for the Mighty One has done great things for me—holy is his name.

NARRATOR 2: Mary stayed with Elizabeth for three months.

*(Suggested drama:* A Carpenter's Rule*)*

NARRATOR 1: In those days Caesar Augustus issued a decree that a census should be taken of the entire Roman world. And everyone went to his own town to register.

NARRATOR 2: So Joseph also went up from the town of Nazareth in Galilee to Judea, to Bethlehem the town of David, because he belonged to the house and line of David. NARRATOR 1: He went there to register with Mary, who was pledged to be married to him and was expecting a child.

NARRATOR 1 / 2: While they were there, the time came for the baby to be born, and she gave birth to her firstborn, a son.

NARRATOR 1: She wrapped him in swaddling clothes and placed him in a manger, because there was no room for them in the inn.

(*Suggested song:* Away in a Manger)

(*Suggested drama:* The Innkeeper's Wife)

NARRATOR 2: And there were shepherds living out in the fields nearby, keeping watch over their flocks at night. An angel of the Lord appeared to them, and the glory of the Lord shone around them, and they were terrified.

ANGEL 2: Do not be afraid. I bring you good news of great joy that will be for all the people. Today in the town of David a Savior has been born to you; he is Christ the Lord. This will be a sign to you: You will find a baby wrapped in cloths and lying in a manger.

ANGEL CHOIR: Glory to God in the highest and on earth peace to men on whom his favor rests.

(*Suggested congregational song:* Angels We Have Heard on High)

SHEPHERD: Let's go to Bethlehem and see this thing that has happened, which the Lord has told us about.

NARRATOR 1: So the shepherds hurried off and found Mary and Joseph, and the baby, who was lying in the manger.

(*Suggested drama:* The Shepherd)

NARRATOR 2: After Jesus was born in Bethlehem in Judea, during the time of King Herod, Magi from the east came to Jerusalem.

MAGI 1: Where is the one who has been born king of the Jews?

MAGI 2: We saw his star in the east.

MAGI 3: We have come to worship him.

(*Suggested song:* We Three Kings)

NARRATOR 1: When King Herod heard this he was disturbed, and all Jerusalem with him. He had called together all the people's chief priests and teachers of the law.

HEROD: Where is the Christ to be born?

TEACHER 1: In Bethlehem in Judea, for this is what the prophet has written,

TEACHER 2: "But you, Bethlehem, in the land of Judah, are by no means least among the rulers of Judah; for out of you will come a ruler who will be the shepherd of my people Israel."

NARRATOR 2: Then Herod called the Magi secretly and found out from them the exact time the star had appeared. He sent them on to Bethlehem.

HEROD: Go and make a careful search for the child. As soon as you find him, report to me, so that I too may go and worship him.

NARRATOR 1: And the star they had seen in the east went ahead of the Magi until it stopped over the place where the child was.

NARRATOR 2: On coming to the house, they saw the child with his mother Mary.

NARRATOR 1 / 2: . . . And they bowed down and worshiped him.

*(Suggested drama:* Second Chances*)*

*(Suggested song:* O Come, All Ye Faithful*)*